ILLUMINATING VERONICA

Rogelio Martinez

D1560271

BROADWAY PLAY PUBLISHING INC
56 E 81st St., NY NY 10028-0202
212 772-8334 fax: 212 772-8358
BroadwayPlayPubl.com

ILLUMINATING VERONICA
© Copyright 2008 by Rogelio Martinwz

An earlier version of this play was published by Broadway Play Publishing Inc in June 2000 in a collection entitled PLAYS FROM SOUTH COAST REPERTORY: HISPANIC PLAYWRIGHTS PROJECT.

First printing, this edition: December 2008
I S B N: 0-88145-410-9

Book design: Marie Donovan
Word processing: Microsoft Word
Typographic controls: Ventura Publisher
Typeface: Palatino
Printed and bound in the U S A

ABOUT THE AUTHOR

Plays include WHEN TANG MET LAIKA (Sloan Grant/Denver Center/Perry Mansfield), ALL EYES AND EARS (INTAR), FIZZ (N E A/T C G grant/Besch Solinger Productions at the Ohio Theater), LEARNING CURVE (Smith and Krauss New Playwrights: Best Plays of 2005/Besch Solinger Productions at Theater Row), I REGRET SHE'S MADE OF SUGAR (Princess Grace Award), ARRIVALS AND DEPARTURES (Summer Play Festival), and UNION CITY... (E S T, winner of the James Hammerstein Award). In addition, his work has been developed and presented at the Public Theater, Oregon Shakespeare Festival, Mark Taper Forum, and the Magic Theater, among others. Mr Martinez is an alumnus of New Dramatists. He has been commissioned to write a new play by the Atlantic Theater Company and the Arden Theater Company. Mr Martinez teaches playwriting at Goddard College, Montclair University, and Primary Stages. In addition, he runs the Hispanic Playwrights in Residence Lab at INTAR, and is a member of the Dorothy Strelsin Writer's Group at Primary Stages. Mr Martinez was born in Sancti-Spiritus, Cuba, and came to the U S in 1980 on the Mariel boatlift.

ILLUMINATING VERONICA received a workshop
at South Coast Repertory as part of their Pacific
Playwrights Festival.

CHARACTERS & SETTING

VERONICA, *early twenties*
ROSARIO, *her former maid*
MANUEL, *her husband*
PEPIN, *a government official*
SONIA, *a young woman from the provinces*
ERNESTO, *her grandfather*

Place: Havana, Cuba

Time: December 1960-1961

ACT ONE

Scene One

(A room off the entrance to the house. There are several giant bookcases overflowing with books. To the side there is a large window with its curtains pulled closed. The window faces the street. A classical painting hangs on the back wall. In it, a pair of young lovers find each other alone in a garden. The centerpiece of the set is a very old chandelier, probably one of the first models to be powered by electricity.)

(Evening. ROSARIO is standing on a chair trying to dust the chandelier. Unaware that ROSARIO is there, VERONICA enters reading a book. A piece of glass falls off the chandelier and breaks.)

VERONICA: What are you doing here?

ROSARIO: I'll go see if Carlito can fix it.

VERONICA: Carlito left six months ago.

ROSARIO: I forgot.

VERONICA: You don't work here anymore.

ROSARIO: I miss you, Veronica.

VERONICA: I've invited you over for café three times.

ROSARIO: I don't miss your café.

VERONICA: Come. Get down.

ROSARIO: You can't make me not work.

VERONICA: There's no work for you here. I do all the cleaning now.

ROSARIO: You're not very good at it.

VERONICA: I'm doing a perfectly fine job.

ROSARIO: A perfectly fine job doesn't mean you're doing a good job.

VERONICA: Come. Before you fall down.

ROSARIO: The first day it was brought in, there was so much excitement. We waited all morning. It was a Saturday. They promised they would come at nine. It was noon and they hadn't shown up. Finally it arrived. And even though it was new, your father insisted I get up on a chair and dust it anyway.

VERONICA: It's beautiful.

ROSARIO: Isn't it.

VERONICA: Get down. I want to show you something.

ROSARIO: You're not going to try to frighten me the way you used to when you were a child.

VERONICA: No. Look what I have. *(She shows him the book she has been reading.)* Lenin!

ROSARIO: *Ahhhhhhhh!*

VERONICA: What's wrong?

ROSARIO: It's because of that bald-headed Communist I don't work here anymore.

VERONICA: Doesn't Lenin look just like Yul Brynner?

ROSARIO: Are you kidding?

VERONICA: I'm in love with him. Passion and intellect.

ROSARIO: Impossible to find that combination in one man.

VERONICA: Fidel!

ROSARIO: Too hairy.

(VERONICA *gets up on the chair and starts dusting.*)

ROSARIO: What are you doing? What if you fall?

VERONICA: I'll get up again. Sometimes I think you're ridiculous.

(*Pause*)

ROSARIO: You're pregnant.

VERONICA: How did you know?

(ROSARIO *smiles.*)

ROSARIO: Congratulations.

VERONICA: I'm so happy.

ROSARIO: Take advantage of it. If you're tired lie down. Stop whatever you're doing and close your eyes.

VERONICA: I need work to find fulfillment.

ROSARIO: Fulfillment?

VERONICA: Is this better?

ROSARIO: Let me do it.

VERONICA: Never mind. Just read the book.

ROSARIO: I can't. I don't know how.

VERONICA: Of course you can.

ROSARIO: What is it?

VERONICA: Letters from Lenin to Gorky.

ROSARIO: Oh, God. You've really gone nuts.

VERONICA: This is a new world.

ROSARIO: It's the same world. People now use different words to get what they want.

VERONICA: Rosario.

ROSARIO: Just because a boring old Russian wrote it doesn't mean it's any good.

VERONICA: I read Marx too.

ROSARIO: A boring old German. What is wrong with you?

VERONICA: Are you reading?

ROSARIO: Veronica, the floor is dirty.

VERONICA: Stop walking with your head down. There's a lot more going on than dirty floors.

ROSARIO: You need me.

VERONICA: Yes. As a friend.

ROSARIO: No. You can't live without me.

VERONICA: I already do.

ROSARIO: You get lost when you leave the house.

VERONICA: Who told you that?

ROSARIO: A friend saw you the other day wandering aimlessly through the streets. True?

VERONICA: I was gone for four hours. I was eight blocks away, but I didn't know how to get back.

ROSARIO: You have to ask directions.

VERONICA: I don't know east from west.

ROSARIO: Just have them point.

VERONICA: Everyone seems to have a purpose nowadays—some kind of place they need to get to in a hurry. I don't want to get in the way.

(ROSARIO *looks around the room.*)

ROSARIO: I can't believe I lived here once. This was my home, too.

VERONICA: You can come back any time you want. But as a friend.

ROSARIO: Don't let this place fall apart.

VERONICA: I've watched you my whole life. I know how to take care of this house.

ROSARIO: If your father could see you now he'd fall over and die. You never picked up after yourself and now you take care of a whole house.

VERONICA: I do the wash as well.

ROSARIO: Really?

VERONICA: I didn't know washing clothes could be so fulfilling.

ROSARIO: There you go again with this fulfillment thing. How much fulfillment does one person really need? Here. You take the book. Let's have life back as it was. At least in this house...this room.

VERONICA: I refuse to exploit you.

ROSARIO: Exploit me! Exploit me. Go on! Just do something with me.

VERONICA: The person I used to be—I'm a new person. And it's about time you see that. Now I want you as a friend. Just that. Nothing more. Understand? You need to accept that.

(ROSARIO *watches* VERONICA *work. After a moment...)*

ROSARIO: It's hard to go home every night. I liked living here.

VERONICA: It's only normal to go home to your own family.

ROSARIO: When you take care of another family your whole life, your own family forgets you.

VERONICA: Is something wrong?

ROSARIO: My husband has a girlfriend. Petuca.

VERONICA: Who?

ROSARIO: Petuca. The one who used to live on San Cristobal.

VERONICA: I think I know who you're talking about.

ROSARIO: She's moved in.

VERONICA: Where?

ROSARIO: With us.

VERONICA: She's moved in with you?

ROSARIO: For a month now. This is all new for us— for you and me and Petuca. This is a whole new world and I don't know the rules. You should see us at home. We sit around the table—like a family. I sit at one end of the table, Petuca at the other and Tomas between us. In the center. He loves it.

VERONICA: You allow this?

ROSARIO: That's a revolution for you. My husband asked a woman to move in with us and you're cleaning your own house.

VERONICA: Not the same thing.

ROSARIO: Either way, I'm having trouble fitting in. I don't know what to do with the rest of my life.

VERONICA: You can't move back in.

ROSARIO: Why not?

VERONICA: This was your prison. If you move back in, all you'll do is housework day in, day out.

ROSARIO: What do you think my husband expects me to do at home? A revolution has occurred but someone forgot to tell all the men.

VERONICA: You must get Tomas to read Marx—

ROSARIO: He has two women to deal with—and God knows how many that I don't know about...don't want to know—do you think he's going to stop all that to read Marx?

VERONICA: Rosario, do you still...

ROSARIO: What?

VERONICA: You know...

ROSARIO: Are you asking me if I still have sex with my husband?

VERONICA: Yes.

ROSARIO: Ay, Veronica!

VERONICA: I ask...demand it every night.

ROSARIO: You're still so young.

VERONICA: No! No! Listen. The revolution has now given us the right to demand sex from our husbands.

ROSARIO: Not all of us still want to have sex with our husbands.

VERONICA: You don't?

ROSARIO: What am I saying? I do. I'm actually very confused about what I want and no book of yours is going to make me understand this world any better.

VERONICA: You're very pretty. I want you to know that—even if he doesn't tell you....

ROSARIO: When you look at me you only see the past.

VERONICA: I used to want to look like you when I was young. I thought you were the most glamorous woman I knew.

ROSARIO: I was the maid.

VERONICA: You did it with such...such...such flair.

ROSARIO: Now I work in a tobacco factory with hundreds of other women. I miss your father. I miss working for him. I miss running this house.

VERONICA: Now you're part of something larger.

ROSARIO: What?

VERONICA: Communism. This revolution is all about us getting what we want finally. It's about labor. About women's rights. It's about sex.

ROSARIO: Silly.

VERONICA: Everything will change. Fidel at least understands our place in this society.

ROSARIO: In the bed or in the kitchen.

VERONICA: You're too cynical.

ROSARIO: I've lived through too many promises.

(VERONICA *grabs another book.*)

VERONICA: This is Fourier.

ROSARIO: Who?

VERONICA: Very important man.

ROSARIO: Yeah, but who is he?

VERONICA: Very important man. Now listen. "In any given society the degree of woman's emancipation is the natural measure of the general emancipation." One of these days I'm going to throw out all of my father's old books and replace them with books like this one.

ROSARIO: It's just words.

VERONICA: Fidel reads all the time. He's probably already read this one. Take this copy. Have your husband's girlfriend read it to you.

ROSARIO: Will it get me back my husband?

VERONICA: It will teach both of you how to survive without him.

ROSARIO: I already do.

VERONICA: What's that smile about?

ROSARIO: People forget this country already had one revolution.

VERONICA: What do you mean?

ROSARIO: I live on Avenida Camilo Cienfuegos. Two years ago the same street used to be Avenida Narcisso Lopez. One nineteenth century revolutionary leader replaced by a twentieth century one. And so I just wait for a new set of promises to be broken.

(MANUEL *enters carrying a stack of books.*)

MANUEL: Rosario.

VERONICA: About time.

(VERONICA *is still standing on the chair.* MANUEL *walks over to her.*)

MANUEL: I can see up your skirt.

ROSARIO: Oh, how long it's been since a man has wanted to look up my skirt.

MANUEL: So much promise under this skirt.

VERONICA: Naughty.

(VERONICA *kisses* MANUEL. *Some of the books fall to the ground. All three get on the floor and begin to pick them up.*)

ROSARIO: All these books—

MANUEL: I have a lot of work.

ROSARIO: I should go.

VERONICA: Are you coming on Saturday?

ROSARIO: Where?

VERONICA: To help with the harvest. Fidel is counting on all of us.

ROSARIO: Not on you.

VERONICA: Sure. Why not? I have Papi's old machete.

ROSARIO: You can't lift that old thing.

VERONICA: I do. Every night before I fall asleep I lift it several times—and when I wake up, it's the first thing I do. Whenever I have a moment I practice my machete swing. Do you want to see?

ROSARIO: Good night.

VERONICA: No. Stay. Have dinner with us.

ROSARIO: I have to be loyal to my husband's mistress. She gets very upset when I don't come home for dinner.

MANUEL: What?

ROSARIO: She'll explain. *(She starts to go.)*

VERONICA: Are you sure?

ROSARIO: I'll come by again soon. I promise.

VERONICA: It means a lot to me that you came by finally.

ROSARIO: Next time I'll walk you around the block and show you where you live.

(The two women kiss. ROSARIO starts to exit followed by VERONICA.)

ROSARIO: You don't have to show me out. This was once my home, remember? *(She looks around the room one last time and then quickly exits.)*

MANUEL: You have to let go.

VERONICA: What do you mean?

MANUEL: She wanted to go home.

VERONICA: I hadn't seen her in months.

MANUEL: And you think you're friends?

VERONICA: The best of friends.

MANUEL: She worked for you.

VERONICA: We can't be friends?

MANUEL: No. *(He is picking up the remaining books.)*

VERONICA: Why not?

MANUEL: What?

VERONICA: You said we can't be friends. I'd like to know why not?

MANUEL: There are differences. You were her employer.

VERONICA: I let you marry me and you were a bellboy in my father's hotel.

MANUEL: That's different, isn't it?

VERONICA: How?

MANUEL: Love.

VERONICA: Yes. It does complicate matters. *(She kisses him.)* What happened today?

MANUEL: Later.

VERONICA: I want to know now.

MANUEL: We'll talk later. I want to catch the ball game. *(He starts to exit.)*

VERONICA: What's it like out there?

MANUEL: I'll tell you all about it—

VERONICA: Now.

(MANUEL stops.)

MANUEL: I go to work and everyone around me is running around doing their own thing—but with a strong sense of purpose. All of us have the same goal. Survival.

VERONICA: Survival?

MANUEL: At any moment the Americans will attack.

VERONICA: And we're ready.

MANUEL: There are terrible things, too.

VERONICA: Like what?

MANUEL: I don't want to tell you—

VERONICA: What happened?

(Pause)

MANUEL: They shot several men today.

VERONICA: Really?

MANUEL: At the stadium. All of us in the office went during lunch.

VERONICA: You saw the men shot? What was it like?

MANUEL: All their former employees were there denouncing them. We booed and yelled and ate our lunch. Ordinary and extraordinary—

VERONICA: No. What was it like when they—*bang!* *(She laughs.)*

MANUEL: It's not funny.

VERONICA: I know.

MANUEL: This is very serious.

VERONICA: What's going on?

MANUEL: Nothing.

VERONICA: So then. What happened?

MANUEL: I closed my eyes.

VERONICA: Oh, what good are you!

MANUEL: I'll keep them open next time.

VERONICA: There isn't going to be a next time.

MANUEL: Yes. The day after tomorrow.

VERONICA: Can I go?

MANUEL: Of course not. I don't want you having nightmares afterwards. *(He notices the broken glass on the floor.)* Everything is falling apart. I should take it down before it falls on top of us.

VERONICA: It's part of my family's history.

MANUEL: Where are they now?

VERONICA: That's not the point.

MANUEL: They left you. They left all this behind.

VERONICA: Not for lack of trying. If my father could have taken this whole house with him, he would have.

MANUEL: And we should have joined him.

VERONICA: Why do you say that now?

MANUEL: It doesn't matter.

VERONICA: What is it?

MANUEL: I'm starting to see the world...the way it works. Strangers walk by and see a place like this.... We're making the rules up as we go along—nothing would surprise me.

VERONICA: You're not making any sense.

MANUEL: Never mind.

VERONICA: Come here.

MANUEL: What?

(VERONICA kisses MANUEL.)

VERONICA: Longer.

(MANUEL *kisses* VERONICA *longer.*)

VERONICA: No. Your beard, silly. I want you to grow it longer.

MANUEL: You don't like the way I look.

VERONICA: It's not long enough.

MANUEL: I'm not doing this because you know who—

VERONICA: That's what all the men say.

MANUEL: I want—

(VERONICA *kisses* MANUEL *again. Slowly, she reaches into his pocket and takes out a letter.*)

VERONICA: What's this?

MANUEL: I was going to show you.

(VERONICA *looks at the letter.*)

VERONICA: From my father.

MANUEL: Yes.

VERONICA: You read it.

MANUEL: I didn't think you'd mind.

VERONICA: I like to open my own letters.

MANUEL: It was already open. A man brought it by work.

VERONICA: I don't understand.

MANUEL: They're watching you.

VERONICA: Who?

MANUEL: It's nothing to worry about—

VERONICA: I'm being watched but I shouldn't worry.

MANUEL: It's going to be okay.

VERONICA: Who read the letter?

MANUEL: It's from your father. Telling you how life there is—he has a new Cadillac.

VERONICA: As if that's what life is.

MANUEL: This is not the first letter you've received from Miami.

VERONICA: I don't write back.

MANUEL: They can't understand why you stayed. You were from a different class. Your whole family— all your friends left. Your life went with them.

VERONICA: You are my life.

MANUEL: I know but...

VERONICA: What?

MANUEL: We...we both could have started over. Your father has the money and—

VERONICA: We decided.

MANUEL: You decided for us. Look, it doesn't matter now. What's done is done.

VERONICA: Then why do you insist on talking about it.

MANUEL: Is the shower working?

VERONICA: The shower is working but there's no water.

MANUEL: I'll try to fix it. (*He starts to go.*)

VERONICA: I want to be a part of this

MANUEL: We don't have a choice now, do we?

VERONICA: Why are they looking at my letters?

MANUEL: They don't trust you. They think you're a spy.

VERONICA: Oh, now that's the silliest thing I've ever heard.

MANUEL: Everyone is spying on everyone else. The C I A and the K G B are both here—probably wandering this very street right now. Just the other night one of Fidel's cigars exploded. A janitor had stolen it from his office. He was found dead with his head—well... Messy.

VERONICA: And no janitor to clean it up.

MANUEL: Sometimes I don't understand your sense of humor.

VERONICA: Sometimes I don't understand you.

(Pause)

MANUEL: This is not a game. You do see their point.

VERONICA: No. I don't. Do you?

MANUEL: I'm trying to get you to understand.

VERONICA: I'm going to try to hurt—is that it? Me. Look at me? I wouldn't know how.

MANUEL: One learns.

VERONICA: One learns. (She looks inside the letter and finds a check.)

MANUEL: A thousand dollars. Every month he sends you a little more.

VERONICA: The man puts a price on everything. (She puts the check in a little box on one of the bookshelves. Inside the box there are more checks.)

MANUEL: You're not going to cash it? With twins on the way—

VERONICA: We don't need it.

MANUEL: This is our chance.

VERONICA: I know.

MANUEL: Then why do you keep them?

VERONICA: A way of remembering who my family was and why I stayed. (She looks at her father's letter, *but almost immediately throws it away.)* Now tell me everything that happened to you today—and start with the executions.

MANUEL: Shouldn't you read what he wrote?

VERONICA: Not one more word about that letter. Understand?

(MANUEL nods. He hesitates and then...)

MANUEL: I have good news.

VERONICA: You do?

MANUEL: I have all sorts of news.

VERONICA: Why have you waited this long to tell me?

MANUEL: How are the babies? Can they take the shock of good news?

VERONICA: They're tough. Just like their mother.

MANUEL: When are you going to stop acting as if you can do everything?

VERONICA: When you finally accept that I can.

MANUEL: Okay. Do you want to hear the news or not?

VERONICA: *Yes!*

MANUEL: The Associate Minister of Culture told me I was doing an exceptional job.

VERONICA: That's it?

MANUEL: I didn't even think he knew me. Out of the blue he comes up to me and we start talking about baseball. The New York Yankees and how they just lost the Series to the Pirates. He thinks they should come here during the off-season and have Fidel work with them.

VERONICA: Fidel?

MANUEL: He has an incredible fastball. Of course, all the time I'm shaking my head, Yes! Yes! Whatever! I want a promotion. And as he's about to go, he asks me if I would be interested—

VERONICA: In what?

MANUEL: What?

VERONICA: In what?

MANUEL: I'm about to tell you.

VERONICA: Tell me.

MANUEL: In a promotion.

(VERONICA *kisses* MANUEL.)

MANUEL: He likes the reports I've been filing. I have a chance.

VERONICA: Really?

MANUEL: Yeah.

VERONICA: That's great.

MANUEL: I know.

VERONICA: What kind of promotion?

(MANUEL *goes over to the stack of books he carried in with him.*)

MANUEL: These books contain counterrevolutionary elements. He's read them already. He wants to see what I think.

VERONICA: I knew you'd do well there.

MANUEL: I'll be promoted to Editor of Content.

VERONICA: What does that mean?

MANUEL: I have no idea, but it sounds important.

VERONICA: Editor of Content. I like it. I like it a lot.

MANUEL: Me too.

VERONICA: Did they tell you what you would have to do?

MANUEL: I will no longer be just a lowly censor. My job now will be to go through all the books published in the last fifty years and put them in a socialist context.

VERONICA: Rewrite them?

MANUEL: If necessary.

VERONICA: All of them?

MANUEL: Every single one of them.

VERONICA: That's a lot of books.

MANUEL: It's a good thing—means I'll have a job for a while. *(He walks over to the stack of books he carried in.)* The whole lot of them—counter-revolutionary! My reports have to be in by the end of the week. You take half.

VERONICA: I can't wait to get started.

MANUEL: We're going to have to spend extra time going over the ones you read.

VERONICA: I always find everything that's counterrevolutionary in them.

MANUEL: I know. I just...I don't want them to find out.

VERONICA: That your wife is intelligent.

MANUEL: Don't be silly.

VERONICA: I'd do so well there.

MANUEL: I know.

VERONICA: Everything is changing.

MANUEL: Slowly.

VERONICA: When can I join you there?

MANUEL: Soon.

VERONICA: How many women work there?

MANUEL: Three. Four.

VERONICA: What do they do?

MANUEL: One is a secretary.

VERONICA: And the others?

MANUEL: I think they're family of the director.

VERONICA: Fidel is going to put an end to all that corruption.

MANUEL: Yes.

VERONICA: I heard him on the radio. He doesn't want women to just sit home and watch life pass them by. He wants us to participate in the experiment.

MANUEL: What experiment?

VERONICA: Communism. That's how he referred to it on the radio this morning.

MANUEL: As an experiment?

VERONICA: Rosario already works in a tobacco factory.

MANUEL: Rosario worked before the Revolution.

VERONICA: Are you saying I can't?

MANUEL: You'll have your hands full with the twins.

VERONICA: I want to work at the Ministry of Culture with you.

MANUEL: It doesn't happen overnight.

VERONICA: Have you asked your supervisor about it?

MANUEL: Wait until I get this. Then...yes...yes...

VERONICA: I can't keep waiting.

MANUEL: I know.

VERONICA: I want my life to start. *(She looks at one of the books.)* Proust.

MANUEL: Yeah. A new translation. As if we needed the old one.

VERONICA: I loved Proust growing up.

MANUEL: I never read him.

(VERONICA puts down the book and walks over to one of the bookshelves. She gets a book.)

VERONICA: Here it is.

MANUEL: You have a copy of it?

VERONICA: My father's copy. He gave it to me when I turned fifteen. Listen.

MANUEL: You read the whole thing?

VERONICA: I never got past the prologue.

(VERONICA reads. There is a subtle change of light.)

VERONICA: "But for me it was enough if, in my own bed, my sleep was so heavy as completely to relax my consciousness; for then I lost all sense of the place in which I had gone to sleep, and when I awoke at midnight, not knowing where I was, I could not be sure at first who I was; I had only the most rudimentary sense of existence, such as may lurk and flicker in the depths of an animal's consciousness; I was more destitute of human qualities than the cave-dweller; but then the memory, not yet of the place in which I was, but of various other places where I had lived, and might now very possibly be, would come like a rope let down from heaven to draw me up out of the abyss of not-being, from which I could never have escaped by myself...." *(She looks up at MANUEL.)* All of a sudden I miss home.

MANUEL: You are home.

VERONICA: Yes. I know. Isn't that silly?

(MANUEL *looks down at the copy he brought in.*)

MANUEL: *Remembrance of Things Past.*

(VERONICA *continues to look at the book.*)

MANUEL: The title alone is counterrevolutionary.

VERONICA: Why?

MANUEL: Now. This. The present. To the Revolution that's all that matters. The past is not worth remembering.

VERONICA: He writes with beauty and grace.

MANUEL: And uses too many words. Look at this. There are two more volumes. No, three. *Four!* Why wasn't this man stopped.

(VERONICA *puts her copy of Proust back on the bookshelf.*)

VERONICA: I can't wait to begin. We'll start tonight. *(She kisses him.)* Sweet.

MANUEL: Veronica?

VERONICA: What?

MANUEL: Why was Rosario here tonight?

VERONICA: She thinks this is still her home.

MANUEL: I want you to be careful. You don't know whose side people are on.

VERONICA: I know.

MANUEL: Do you?

(VERONICA *nods yes.*)

VERONICA: We'll get started immediately after dinner.

MANUEL: Good.

VERONICA: Thank you.

MANUEL: Why?

VERONICA: I don't know. I suddenly felt like saying that.

(*Suddenly an air raid siren.* MANUEL *and* VERONICA *panic. He looks outside.*)

MANUEL: Get the lights.

VERONICA: Do you see anything?

MANUEL: All the lights are out.

VERONICA: Hurry. They're bombing us. Get under here.

(MANUEL *and* VERONICA *get under a table—like two children.*)

MANUEL: Do you think getting under this table will protect us from American bombs?

VERONICA: This is what Fidel tells us to do. I saw him demonstrate it on T V.

MANUEL: I don't want you to watch so much television.

VERONICA: Why not?

MANUEL: All that's on is Fidel.

VERONICA: That's all I'm interested in.

MANUEL: Switch the channel next time he's on.

VERONICA: When he comes on, both stations carry him.

MANUEL: Then just turn it off.

VERONICA: Was that a bomb?

MANUEL: No. Are you listening to me?

(*Pause*)

VERONICA: Why do you come home so late?

MANUEL: I have a lot of work.

VERONICA: Titi's husband gets home around seven every night.

MANUEL: Titi's husband is not getting a promotion, is he?

VERONICA: I miss you all day.

(Pause)

MANUEL: I bet it's a false alarm.

VERONICA: The lights are out.

MANUEL: Yes.

VERONICA: Maybe you want to make love to me.

MANUEL: It's a false alarm every day.

VERONICA: Make love to me. *(Pause)* I want color.

MANUEL: Color?

VERONICA: I want color television, Manuel.

MANUEL: That doesn't exist.

VERONICA: That man Nixon showed one to the Russians a couple of years ago. Now my father has one over there.

MANUEL: Then that's where you belong. It's where we both belong.

VERONICA: I want color television; I don't want to be over there.

MANUEL: Sometimes you don't get a choice.

(The siren stops. MANUEL gets up from under the table; VERONICA stays under it.)

(After a moment...)

MANUEL: Another false alarm.

(Blackout)

Scene Two

(Two weeks later)

(PEPIN is on stage. He wears a heavily decorated uniform. He looks around the room, pours himself a glass of rum, and makes himself comfortable. After a moment, VERONICA enters.)

VERONICA: There you are. I didn't hear you knock.

PEPIN: I let myself in.

VERONICA: Would you like something to—

(PEPIN points to his drink.)

PEPIN: You don't mind, do you?

VERONICA: My husband will be back soon. Would you like to sit?

PEPIN: I don't have a lot of time.

VERONICA: You're early.

PEPIN: My timing isn't always spot on, Mrs Santiago.

VERONICA: Veronica.

PEPIN: Mrs Santiago, if it's alright with you.

VERONICA: Of course.

PEPIN: I have over sixty men working for me—at least half of them are married. I can't remember the names of all their first wives.

VERONICA: First wives?

PEPIN: Sorry. The first names of all their wives— is that right?

VERONICA: I don't think so.

PEPIN: I give up.

VERONICA: Does my husband have a second wife that I don't know about?

PEPIN: Do you have reason to think so?

VERONICA: No.

PEPIN: Then there you are.

(Neither PEPIN *nor* VERONICA *knows quite what to say next.)*

VERONICA: I didn't expect you in uniform.

PEPIN: Excuse me?

VERONICA: Your uniform.

PEPIN: Oh. Just got this little red star the other day. Come.

*(*VERONICA *steps forward.)*

VERONICA: What did you do to get it?

PEPIN: I saved Fidel's life when we fought together in the Sierra.

VERONICA: You did?

PEPIN: He thinks I did.

VERONICA: Not following you.

PEPIN: I stole books and brought them up to the mountains where he was. Fidel is a very serious reader.

VERONICA: You go from thief to Associate Minister of Culture.

PEPIN: I was very good at what I did. I left little I O Us behind.

VERONICA: Did Fidel pay them back?

PEPIN: Of course. He freed the country.

VERONICA: From what exactly?

PEPIN: People like your father.

VERONICA: Excuse me?

PEPIN: He's not here anymore.

VERONICA: No.

PEPIN: After the Revolution I stayed at your father's hotel. I had never even stepped inside the lobby. I could never walk through the door.

VERONICA: He didn't stop anyone from walking in.

PEPIN: That's true...but he didn't make me feel that I was good enough to enter.

VERONICA: That's your problem, not my father's.

PEPIN: Now I feel good enough.

VERONICA: Well then...it worked out for you.

PEPIN: It did.

(VERONICA *smiles.*)

VERONICA: I like your uniform.

PEPIN: Most women do.

VERONICA: I didn't mean to—

PEPIN: Flattery comes natural to you. You were taught to make strangers feel welcomed.

VERONICA: Yes.

PEPIN: Whores are taught a similar skill. Of course they take it to a different conclusion—or not so different?

VERONICA: Maybe you should come back.

PEPIN: I'm making you uncomfortable.

VERONICA: No. I'm familiar with the word whore. It appears several times in the Communist Manifesto.

PEPIN: I don't think I've read the same translation. *(He looks around the room.)* My children also love the uniform. They can't believe it's daddy wearing it. I raise my voice and they do everything I ask them to do. My own barracks. Even my wife falls into line.

VERONICA: You wear it to bed?

PEPIN: As a matter of fact, I often do—only out of alertness. When the Americans attack—and they will—all I'll have to do is jump out of bed and—

VERONICA: Go steal some books.

(PEPIN looks at VERONICA and smiles.)

PEPIN: You're pregnant.

VERONICA: Three months. Maybe when they get in trouble my husband can borrow your uniform.

PEPIN: They?

VERONICA: Twins.

PEPIN: It's too early to tell.

VERONICA: I broke an egg and there were two yolks in it.

PEPIN: Fair enough.

VERONICA: I have names picked out for them. Fidel and Raul.

PEPIN: What if they're girls?

VERONICA: Girls?

PEPIN: Yes. No one thinks of girls.

VERONICA: You do.

PEPIN: I have to. I have three of my own.

VERONICA: It doesn't matter what they are. They're communists.

PEPIN: You know that for a fact.

VERONICA: For a fact.

PEPIN: It took Fidel almost thirty-four years to admit he was one.

VERONICA: The world moves at a much faster rate now.

PEPIN: How do you keep up? You no longer have three servants to help you.

VERONICA: I do with less.

PEPIN: This is less. What was more?

VERONICA: How did you know that?

PEPIN: That you had three—

VERONICA: Yes.

PEPIN: When your husband came to work for us, we did an extensive background check.

VERONICA: I stayed.

PEPIN: Odd decision considering your whole family—

VERONICA: I have to ask. Before we go on—

PEPIN: What?

VERONICA: I just need to know. Are you here to talk to my husband or to question me?

(Pause)

PEPIN: Your husband.

VERONICA: I don't know where he is. He should be here.

PEPIN: Did he say where he was going?

VERONICA: He comes and goes...he doesn't always tell me.

PEPIN: I can't stay long. In fact, maybe I should—

VERONICA: I'm sure if you wait five more minutes.

(Pause)

PEPIN: You love your husband very much.

VERONICA: I do.

PEPIN: You're in love.

VERONICA: Yes.

PEPIN: It wasn't a question. I can see that. It's obvious.
(Short pause) I'll give you five more minutes.

VERONICA: He'll be happy you waited.

PEPIN: I want to make *you* happy.

(Short pause)

VERONICA: Would you like more—

PEPIN: Just five more minutes.

(Pause)

(PEPIN *studies the painting.*)

VERONICA: Do you like it? It belongs to my aunt.

PEPIN: It belonged.

VERONICA: What?

PEPIN: She left. It doesn't belong to her anymore.
(He examines it further.) It's too bad she didn't take
it with her.

VERONICA: She tried. There was room for either that
painting or her new husband. As I understand it,
the decision was not an easy one.

PEPIN: Lenin says, "It is not enough for revolution that
the exploited should demand changes; what is required
for revolution is that the exploiters should not be able
to live and rule in the old way."

VERONICA: Lenin says that?

PEPIN: This house—that painting for example. Or the furniture—what kind of wood is this?

VERONICA: If you'd like we can wait for my husband in the living room.

PEPIN: This is not the living room?

VERONICA: This is the reading room. I prefer this room but if you'd like—

PEPIN: How many rooms are there in this house?

VERONICA: I don't walk around—

PEPIN: It's a big house.

VERONICA: I suppose but...with children on their way—

PEPIN: Twins.

VERONICA: Yes.

PEPIN: It's still a lot of space.

VERONICA: Yes.

(Short pause)

PEPIN: I'm sure you need it all. *(Pause)* Why don't you take the painting down.

VERONICA: I happen to like it. It's love—the possibility of love as the afternoon slowly fades away.

PEPIN: You believe in the possibility of love?

VERONICA: Of course.

PEPIN: *(Pointing to the painting)* In revolutionary society everything must have one purpose—to make the revolution. That painting is not part of the new world.

VERONICA: It's two lovers—

PEPIN: Obsessed with one another.

VERONICA: What's wrong with that?

PEPIN: Obsession. Love. Whatever you wish to call it. It can stop you from making the right decision.

VERONICA: You do believe in romantic love?

PEPIN: I believe in making the most out of what's thrown my way.

(VERONICA *laughs*.)

VERONICA: It's just a painting.

PEPIN: With very little use in revolutionary society.

VERONICA: The end of romance?

PEPIN: The end of sentimentality. Art is secondary to purpose. Do you understand what that means?

(*Pause*)

VERONICA: I'll take it down. Will you help me?

PEPIN: Of course.

(PEPIN *and* VERONICA *take the painting down*.)

VERONICA: I'm so lucky.

PEPIN: Why?

VERONICA: The Minister of Culture is redecorating my house.

PEPIN: The Associate Minister of Culture. (*He takes out a small knife.*) I've had this since I was five. I used to carve my name on everything. This need of mine. To mark where I've been. (*He gives her the knife.*) Go ahead.

VERONICA: What do I tell her when she returns?

PEPIN: Your aunt?

VERONICA: Yes.

PEPIN: Why would she return?

VERONICA: They say—

PEPIN: Who?

VERONICA: My father says this won't last.

PEPIN: And you believe him?

VERONICA: No.

PEPIN: You're afraid to destroy it because you think they're going to return.

VERONICA: I didn't say that.

PEPIN: You can't live in two worlds.

VERONICA: I don't.

PEPIN: You do. This house is one world, but just outside its doors is another.

VERONICA: I need to sit down.

PEPIN: Are you all right?

(VERONICA sits.)

VERONICA: I don't feel well.

PEPIN: Here. A glass of water.

VERONICA: Thank you.

PEPIN: Can I get you—

(During the following there is a subtle change of light. Schumann plays off in the distance.)

VERONICA: Do you ever get—do you ever remember things from your past. Things you had forgotten. Like a painting has the—to remember what you were like. It happens sometimes when I'm alone. I go into my older sister's room—she has this little music box that I open and Schumann plays. And just as it gets— I think she's going to walk through the door. I wait and I wait but she never comes back.

PEPIN: She isn't returning.

VERONICA: I've spent my whole life in this house.
Do you think they have similar memories?

PEPIN: Who?

VERONICA: My sisters. Do they remember? It takes one
hundred and eighty-six steps from my room to the
front of the house—that is if you cut across the patio.
I just did that again the other day. We used to do that.
When we were learning to count. We'd spend all day
counting steps. Do they remember that?

PEPIN: Find yourself something to do other than count
steps from your room to the front of the house.

VERONICA: I'm trying to.

*(The lights have changed back to normal. Music is no longer
heard.)*

PEPIN: Your husband is about to come back.

VERONICA: Maybe you should go.

PEPIN: I have bad news for him.

VERONICA: You can't—

PEPIN: He didn't get the promotion.

VERONICA: Why?

PEPIN: I didn't think he was trustworthy enough.

VERONICA: He is.

PEPIN: My concern has more to do with you.

VERONICA: With me?

PEPIN: A wife can exert the wrong kind of influence
on her husband.

VERONICA: I want this more than anything.

PEPIN: I don't think you have any idea what you want.

VERONICA: You don't know me.

PEPIN: I'll break the news to him tomorrow. It's best I do it at work. I was curious to see you with my own eyes.

VERONICA: Curious?

PEPIN: He hasn't brought you by work. No one knew what you looked like. *(He gets up to go.)*

VERONICA: Don't go.

PEPIN: Mrs Santiago.

(PEPIN is eye to eye with VERONICA. He kisses her. After a moment, he stops and looks her in the eyes.)

VERONICA: What is it?

PEPIN: That kiss just now proves to me there's a revolutionary inside of you just aching to get out.

VERONICA: I didn't mean to do that.

PEPIN: You can't live in two worlds.

VERONICA: What do you mean?

PEPIN: Lenin.

VERONICA: I don't understand what you want from me.

PEPIN: "It is not enough for revolution that the exploited should demand changes; what is required for revolution is that the exploiters should not be able to live and rule in the old way."

VERONICA: I love my husband.

PEPIN: You can't have revolution under the values taught to you by your father.

VERONICA: What do you want?

PEPIN: For you to prove to me that you can let go of everything you come from.

(VERONICA cuts the painting with the knife.)

VERONICA: Is that enough?

PEPIN: That and more.

(PEPIN *gently takes the knife from* VERONICA's *hand.*)

PEPIN: It is your decision to make.

VERONICA: What?

PEPIN: Whether he gets the promotion or not. I'll stand by your decision. If you want to help your husband, then I'll see you again. Next Tuesday? Your decision.

(PEPIN *exits.* VERONICA *is restless. After a moment,* ROSARIO *enters quickly.* VERONICA *is startled.*)

ROSARIO: I have good news. I came as soon as I found out.

VERONICA: You saw a man on your way in.

ROSARIO: What?

VERONICA: On your way in, did you see someone?

ROSARIO: No. But I have to tell you—

VERONICA: Are you sure?

ROSARIO: The door was open but there wasn't—

VERONICA: He was just here.

ROSARIO: Starting next week I'm your neighbor.

VERONICA: What?

ROSARIO: I'm moving into Mrs Busto's home just down the block.

VERONICA: I don't understand.

ROSARIO: I'm moving into—

VERONICA: Where is she going?

ROSARIO: Veronica.

VERONICA: What?

ROSARIO: She's in jail.

VERONICA: It's still her house.

ROSARIO: I thought you'd be happy for me.

VERONICA: This is not your neighborhood.

ROSARIO: I've lived here almost half my life.

VERONICA: Working for my father. Not the same thing.

ROSARIO: I'm not good enough.

VERONICA: No. Not at all. It's just...it's not your house.

(*Pause*)

ROSARIO: They told me this would happen.

VERONICA: What are you talking about?

ROSARIO: I said no. She reads Marx and thinks Lenin looks like Yul Brynner, but they said to watch and wait.

VERONICA: They?

ROSARIO: The government has me looking at what people do around here.

VERONICA: Gossip.

ROSARIO: Fidel has raised gossip to the level of national security. It is my responsibility to gossip. I love the job. *El Comité de Defensa de la Revolucion.*

VERONICA: Why wouldn't they let me do that?

ROSARIO: Look at how you live.

VERONICA: What do they want? For me to just give it away.

ROSARIO: They can make you do that.

VERONICA: They can?

ROSARIO: Yes.

VERONICA: I was born in this house.

ROSARIO: You're too sentimentally attached to the way things were.

VERONICA: That's not true.

ROSARIO: Your head is in those books you read, but your heart is somewhere in the past.

VERONICA: This doesn't sound like you.

ROSARIO: I'm sorry but I'm just stating the facts. I'll come back another time. *(She starts to exit.)*

VERONICA: I need to know something.

*(*ROSARIO *stops.)*

VERONICA: Did you ever have an affair?

ROSARIO: Of course I had an affair—I had more than one.

VERONICA: You did?

ROSARIO: Everyone did. There was no television in my day.

VERONICA: I didn't think women did that back then.

ROSARIO: The men couldn't do it all by themselves.

VERONICA: Someone told me today that I have to be an adulteress to be truly revolutionary.

ROSARIO: Fidel wants to take credit for everything, but adultery was part of this country long before he was born.

VERONICA: A woman like myself would never have even thought about doing that years ago.

ROSARIO: Yes she would have. You're smart, Veronica, but you don't understand the heart.

VERONICA: Are you having one now?

ROSARIO: An affair takes time and time is something I don't have anymore. I work now more than ever. The

women who have time are women like you—the old
bourgeoisie. The ones still home.

VERONICA: I've never heard you use that word before.

ROSARIO: What word?

VERONICA: The B word. Bourgeo—it's not a nice word
when you use it to refer to me.

ROSARIO: It's the truth.

VERONICA: You don't always have to tell the truth.

ROSARIO: I do now that I work for the government.

VERONICA: Why are you doing this?

ROSARIO: You have faith. When you were little and
you prayed in church I was jealous of you because
I really thought you were talking to God. The way
you squeezed your eyes shut and put your little hands
together. All your life you've had faith. It makes no
difference to you whether it's God or the Revolution,
you're a believer. For me it's simple. I finally get to
be first in line. I've never had that chance.

(MANUEL *enters with a bottle of champagne.*)

MANUEL: Here we are.

(MANUEL *gives a glass to* VERONICA, *takes his glass and
gives it to* ROSARIO.)

ROSARIO: What are we celebrating?

MANUEL: Tell us.

VERONICA: Why are you so late?

MANUEL: What happened?

ROSARIO: Oh, forget it. Plenty to celebrate. Let's just
drink.

VERONICA: Why are you looking at me like that?

MANUEL: A few blocks down I ran into Pepin.

VERONICA: Pepin?

MANUEL: He was just here. The man who had rum in my house—told me how much he liked you.

VERONICA: He did?

ROSARIO: Can I have some more?

MANUEL: He went on and on and on about you. You made quite an impression on him.

ROSARIO: Just a little more. I feel great.

MANUEL: After a moment I couldn't wait any longer. I just had to know if I had the promotion or not. He said to ask you. Why are you so quiet?

VERONICA: I don't know.

MANUEL: Well?

VERONICA: He said I would know?

MANUEL: *(Smiling)* Stop playing games.

VERONICA: But—

MANUEL: You're playing games.

VERONICA: No. I just—

MANUEL: Just tell me now. I can't wait any longer.

ROSARIO: Tell him already. Can I have just a little—

MANUEL: Why are you doing this?

VERONICA: Manuel, I'm sorry—

(MANUEL *grabs hold of* VERONICA *causing her to accidentally drop the glass.)*

MANUEL: *Just tell me.*

(Pause)

VERONICA: *(Matter-of-factly)* You got it.

(MANUEL *hugs* VERONICA. *Then he dances wildly.)*

MANUEL: Of course. Of course, I got it. Of course. I wanted you to say it—just to say the words.

(ROSARIO *pours herself another glass of champagne.*)

ROSARIO: Congratulations.

MANUEL: Sometimes I don't understand you.

VERONICA: I want to understand myself.

(MANUEL *pushes* ROSARIO *out.*)

MANUEL: Take the bottle—the glass. Take it. Take it. Good night.

ROSARIO: I'll come by and see you.

MANUEL: Good night.

VERONICA: Rosario. Is there work for me at the tobacco factory?

MANUEL: You don't have to go to work.

ROSARIO: Nothing right now.

VERONICA: Have you asked?

ROSARIO: Yes.

VERONICA: I thought I'd remind you in case—

ROSARIO: I'll let you know.

VERONICA: I've been reading up on tobacco farming—in case they call me in.

ROSARIO: You don't need to read books to roll tobacco. (*She exits.*)

MANUEL: Tobacco? You don't have to—

VERONICA: I want to.

(MANUEL *looks at the painting.*)

MANUEL: What are you doing with this?

VERONICA: I didn't like it anymore.

MANUEL: You said it was your favorite.

VERONICA: Oh, well. I fell out of love with it.
It happens, you know.

MANUEL: You didn't have to destroy it.

VERONICA: Two years ago my father would have
bought you that job.

MANUEL: And I would have felt terrible about it.

VERONICA: You would have?

MANUEL: It doesn't work that way anymore.

VERONICA: Oh. Explain. How does it work?

MANUEL: Hard work gets you somewhere.

VERONICA: It does?

MANUEL: Why are you upset?

VERONICA: I don't know.

MANUEL: I did this on my own—without your father's
help. Your help—or anyone. On my own.

VERONICA: On your own.

MANUEL: Yes. I know your father is over there starting
a business—telling you I'm not any good.

VERONICA: I don't care.

MANUEL: I know you don't—but after a while you
start to believe him anyway.

VERONICA: No.

MANUEL: This is the first time that—the first time
I believe I deserve you.

VERONICA: What?

MANUEL: Up to now, I didn't really believe I deserved
you.

VERONICA: How can you think that way?

MANUEL: I loved you but I didn't think I was good enough for you. I worked for your father—a bellboy... do you know what that is. My eyes looking down at the floor all day. You do that long enough you can't help start to believe that's who you are.

VERONICA: But you're so much more than that.

MANUEL: Yes. I am. Look what I'm doing with my life now.

VERONICA: And me?

MANUEL: What about you?

VERONICA: Exactly. What happens to me when you leave for work? I'm still a housewife with two children on their way.

MANUEL: We both wanted—you insisted on staying.

VERONICA: Every day I sit at home. In the morning after you go, I do the wash. Then I move to the kitchen, the dishes, the silverware, that night's meal; and with all the cleaning afterwards, it isn't until noon that I realize I'm not going anywhere. That this is it.

MANUEL: I wanted to leave the country with your father, but you insisted on staying. Make up your mind finally. What do you want?

VERONICA: To be taken seriously.

MANUEL: I take you seriously.

VERONICA: Why can't you tell them I do half your work? Why can't I work with you.

MANUEL: It takes time.

VERONICA: Tell them I write those reports.

MANUEL: You help me to write—

VERONICA: I write them. *(Pause)* I'm going to the
movies. I haven't left the house all day.

MANUEL: Sure. Let me go wash up—

VERONICA: Alone.

MANUEL: Why don't you ask Rosario if—

VERONICA: Alone.

(Pause)

MANUEL: I'll let Pepin know you want to work.
All right? I promise.

VERONICA: You will?

MANUEL: Yes.

VERONICA: I think he's going to start coming around
more often.

MANUEL: He said that?

VERONICA: In a way.

MANUEL: I hope you're right. I really do. It'll change
our life.

VERONICA: It already has.

MANUEL: Of course it has.

*(MANUEL kisses VERONICA but she doesn't respond.
He lets her go. She's about to exit.)*

MANUEL: Veronica. How will you know how to get
back?

VERONICA: I'll ask a stranger for directions. *(She exits.)*

*(MANUEL is left on stage. After a moment he walks over to
the painting. He runs his fingers down the slash.)*

(Lights fade to black.)

END OF ACT ONE

ACT TWO

Scene One

(A few weeks later)

(There's a picture of Fidel Castro where the painting used to hang.)

(VERONICA enters nervously. She notices the picture of Fidel and walks right up to it.)

VERONICA: Call me old fashioned but I don't like to be watched. What's about to happen here is none of your business. *(She turns the picture over.)*

(Standing at the entrance to the room is PEPIN.)

PEPIN: What's about to happen?

VERONICA: I don't know why you bother to wear a uniform if you're just going to take it off the moment you walk in.

PEPIN: Formality.

VERONICA: For this?

PEPIN: I imagine a day when we just talk.

VERONICA: You do?

PEPIN: Yes. I walk in. We sit drinking café, chatting about politics. My uniform doesn't always have to come off.

VERONICA: Let me go make some café then.

PEPIN: I said I imagine a day.

VERONICA: Ah.

PEPIN: I left it open for the possibility of us having something other than sex.

VERONICA: Not today?

PEPIN: No. I'm afraid today the uniform comes off.

VERONICA: When then? When I'm old and gray? When you've moved on?

PEPIN: You're full of questions.

VERONICA: You have no answers. Why are you smiling?

PEPIN: I can't think until after sex.

VERONICA: My husband says the same thing; then he falls asleep afterwards and never lets me in on the thinking. *(Pause)* I'm sorry. I just wanted to talk.

PEPIN: Try your husband.

VERONICA: I can't. He's never home—but you know that.

PEPIN: This conversation is not going the way I expected.

VERONICA: You didn't expect a conversation.

PEPIN: Let's just try again next Tuesday.

VERONICA: You wouldn't be able to think for a whole week. It would paralyze the Ministry of Culture. The country would have no culture for an entire week just because I didn't lie back and do my revolutionary duty.

PEPIN: Goodbye.

(VERONICA stops PEPIN from leaving.)

VERONICA: You really can't stand the fact you're having sex with me.

PEPIN: What?

VERONICA: Old society.

PEPIN: Why do you say that?

VERONICA: You don't look at me afterwards. You can't stand me.

PEPIN: I'm selfish in bed. You're not the first one to point that out—don't make it anymore complicated than it is. *(He kisses her and starts to go. He stops and returns. He turns the picture of Fidel back over.)* I've been here before. This room. Once.

VERONICA: What do you mean?

PEPIN: I knew your family.

VERONICA: You did?

PEPIN: I went to the University of Havana with your sister Ana Gloria. We studied music history together. Mostly we studied opera.

VERONICA: That was you.

PEPIN: I was the poor kid that she brought home with her.

VERONICA: You disappeared after that one night.

PEPIN: That night after dinner your father took me aside. He had an envelope with money. He asked me to look inside. The money was mine to take if I never returned.

VERONICA: I'm sure my father put enough money in the envelope to make the decision an easy one.

PEPIN: I walked away. Without the money. I decided that I would one day return...on my own terms. Here I am. *(He puts his hat back on.)*

VERONICA: You don't have to go.

PEPIN: I'm not in a very good mood right now.
(He starts to go.)

VERONICA: I want to come work for you.

PEPIN: You do?

VERONICA: I don't want to be trapped in this house anymore. I want to work.

PEPIN: That's not going to happen.

(Pause)

VERONICA: My husband has asked you.

PEPIN: For a job?

VERONICA: Yes.

PEPIN: For you?

VERONICA: Yes. *(Pause)* He tells me he asks you every day.

PEPIN: You shouldn't believe everything your husband tells you.

VERONICA: Why should I believe you?

PEPIN: I'm not married to you; I've no need to lie to you.

VERONICA: Are you sure he hasn't asked you? Not once? *(Pause)* I'm asking you now.

PEPIN: I'd have to consider this.

VERONICA: What's there to consider?

PEPIN: I'd have to find myself a new Tuesday appointment, and that's becoming more and more difficult with so few of you left.

VERONICA: You're not taking me seriously.

PEPIN: The Ministry is not the right place for you.

VERONICA: Why?

PEPIN: You wouldn't feel comfortable there.

VERONICA: You promised this would free me. All it did was get my husband a job. I'm still home. Waiting.

PEPIN: The truth is that you're going to wait a long time. You don't fit in this society or the last.

VERONICA: What are you going to do with me?

PEPIN: I really should go.

VERONICA: What's going to happen to me?

PEPIN: Our good society is changing before our very eyes. Some of you leave the country, others are arrested, and others just die.... Every day there are fewer of you.

VERONICA: I stayed—

PEPIN: This country tolerates you; don't ask anything more of it.

VERONICA: You're going to watch me rot in this house—some kind of punishment for crimes I didn't commit.

PEPIN: This is not a bad house to rot in.

VERONICA: This isn't even my house. Everything in it belongs to my father.

PEPIN: There you go again making the same mistake. Nothing here belongs to your father or to you for that matter. We can come and take it from you at any moment.

VERONICA: My father—everything he taught me— grace, elegance, submission—everything he taught me was wrong. I don't have to live like that—to please anyone anymore. I've read Marx. New ideas. Fulfillment. Equality. Strength. These new ideas have taken hold of me—filled me. I don't ever see me letting them go.

PEPIN: You have really missed the point.

VERONICA: I don't understand.

PEPIN: You've made this revolution all about yourself. What you want. What you need. Do you really want to understand Marx? There's only one question you have to ask yourself. What purpose do I serve? Clearly, we both know what it is, don't we? (*He is almost at the door to the room.*)

VERONICA: I do half my husband's work. There are days I do it all. His reports—I'm responsible.

PEPIN: What do you mean?

VERONICA: I do—

PEPIN: You don't want to do this to your husband.

VERONICA: He lied to me.

PEPIN: He's your one connection to this new society— the only one keeping you alive around here.

(*Pause*)

VERONICA: He lied to me. Those reports that are so well written...that have allowed him to advance so quickly. You think my husband has the intellect to understand this society. Not a chance.

PEPIN: Mrs Santiago, let me just walk away.

VERONICA: My husband is not smart enough, or for that matter cruel enough, to send artists away—to censor. To do what needs to be done. I can be cruel, Pepin. It's just that up to now I've used my husband to do it. Do you want me to be cruel?

PEPIN: I asked you not to tell me the truth. I like you. I liked coming here. You had one purpose in this revolution. You've just betrayed your only purpose. There's really nothing I can do to save you now.

VERONICA: I'm coming to work with you.

(PEPIN *starts to open the curtains.*)

PEPIN: I wonder just how many people walk by this house every day wanting to know what's inside. What kind of little secrets are buried in here. Who lives here.

(PEPIN *opens the window. For the first time in the play, the outside world is heard. People. Cars. The hustle and bustle of Havana.*)

PEPIN: When we have sex, it always feels like the middle of the night. Then I go out into the day and I'm thrown off. Particularly on a day like today. As I walk down the street, people come right up to me and salute me. They don't know I'm just a bureaucrat. When I leave your house, I feel complete. I walk out into the street, and I think they're saluting me for just having fucked you—for having fucked the old world, old society. The world that tried to bribe me from entering it. This house has remained impenetrable until now. I guess that's what a revolution is. Opening doors. Walking in and doing whatever the hell you want.

(PEPIN *begins to kiss* VERONICA *in front of the window— a humiliating kiss.*)

VERONICA: What are you doing? Not in front of the window. (*She begins to undo her dress.*)

PEPIN: No. I don't want that. I've already had that.

VERONICA: What?

(PEPIN *walks over to the bookshelf and looks at the books.*)

PEPIN: Proust.

VERONICA: Yes. It's my father's—what are you going to do?

PEPIN: It's the old world. It must go. You must go.

(PEPIN *starts to toss the books. At first this surprises*
VERONICA. *She joins him in emptying her father's*
bookshelves. It's violent. She laughs. He laughs. She
stops and realizes the seriousness of the situation.)

PEPIN: You want adventure, Mrs Santiago? You're
going to get real adventure.

(Lights fade to black.)

Scene Two

(A few months later. After the Bay of Pigs)

(All the books are gone. The chandelier is covered with a
white sheet.)

(MANUEL walks around holding a small radio. He's trying
to pick up a signal from an American radio station. Soon
he finds himself holding the radio at arm's length. It looks
awkward and uncomfortable. We're able to hear that the
Bay of Pigs has already happened and that Kennedy is
frustrated with the problem of Cuba.)

(VERONICA enters. She is visibly pregnant. MANUEL turns
off the radio immediately.)

VERONICA: What are you doing?

MANUEL: Nothing. I was just...

VERONICA: They're here.

MANUEL: That's fine.

VERONICA: Come help them bring their bags in.

MANUEL: They had no trouble getting here.

VERONICA: What were you listening to?

MANUEL: The ball game.

VERONICA: Season hasn't started.

MANUEL: I know but—

VERONICA: You think you're a good liar...you're not.

MANUEL: The Americans are not going to let this go on forever. They're going to put an end to it.

(SONIA *and her grandfather,* ERNESTO, *are heard offstage.*)

SONIA: *(Offstage)* Hello? Anyone!

VERONICA: *(calling out)* We're in here.

(SONIA *and her grandfather,* ERNESTO, *enter the room, dragging old luggage with them. They are peasants.*)

ERNESTO: Sorry. Are we—

VERONICA: No. No. Come in. Here. Let me help you.

ERNESTO: I'll just put it here for now.

VERONICA: How was your trip?

SONIA: Lousy.

VERONICA: I'm sorry.

SONIA: This is our house now?

MANUEL: It's not all yours—

ERNESTO: I saw another living room near the entrance.

VERONICA: We prefer this room because it faces the street. It's less private but there's more light.

ERNESTO: Enough rooms to get lost in.

MANUEL: It's not all yours.

SONIA: You just said that.

MANUEL: I wasn't sure you heard me.

VERONICA: This is my husband, Manuel.

SONIA: Sonia. My grandfather, Ernesto.

VERONICA: Veronica.

(MANUEL *takes out some papers.*)

MANUEL: I think we should look at the plans they sent us.

VERONICA: Let me make café.

MANUEL: Let's get this settled first.

SONIA: No hurry. We're not going anywhere. I love the neighborhood.

(*Suddenly, the lights go out.*)

SONIA: Blackouts. How exciting.

MANUEL: Get used to it. (*He gets candles.*)

ERNESTO: Does this happen a lot?

VERONICA: Fidel turns off the lights so Americans can't hit their targets.

SONIA: I didn't know we were moving into a target.

VERONICA: If it were up to my father, he would have bombed this house already.

(MANUEL *lights a candle.*)

ERNESTO: Your father left?

VERONICA: That surprises you?

ERNESTO: No.

VERONICA: That I stayed?

SONIA: You were in love.

VERONICA: You're very clever.

MANUEL: This shows which rooms are for you and what is off limits—ahhh.

VERONICA: Hot wax.

MANUEL: Yes.

VERONICA: Too bad.

SONIA: Want me to hold it?

VERONICA: He has a lot to make up for. Let him hold it.

(SONIA *wanders over to the chandelier. She peeks under the white sheet.*)

SONIA: Aren't you afraid of ghosts?

VERONICA: Ghosts?

SONIA: It's hard to get rid of them.

VERONICA: I haven't seen one.

SONIA: Once they move in, it's almost impossible to get them to move out.

MANUEL: A glass of water near your bed.

SONIA: Yes. Most of the time they're just thirsty.

ERNESTO: Or hungry.

VERONICA: I really wouldn't know. It's not something I believe in.

SONIA: Am I frightening you?

VERONICA: Of course not.

SONIA: We'll start tomorrow. A glass of water in every room of the house. Why is it covered?

VERONICA: I didn't like it.

ERNESTO: What happened to all the books?

VERONICA: I threw them out. Who has time to read?

(MANUEL *points to the map.*)

MANUEL: Let's make sure we understand who gets what?

SONIA: Who gets this room?

VERONICA: It's for all of us to share...if we care to....

SONIA: Good. I was afraid we weren't going to have a reason to run into one another. *(She exits.)*

MANUEL: Where are you going?

ERNESTO: She's restless, you know. Always was.

VERONICA: Would you like something to drink?

ERNESTO: I'm fine. Thanks.

VERONICA: Are you sure? Food?

MANUEL: He said no.

ERNESTO: We had something about an hour ago.

VERONICA: Whatever we have is yours. I won't insist on offering it. From now on, this is your home.

(SONIA enters.)

SONIA: What is that strange thing next to the toilet?

VERONICA: What thing?

SONIA: Next to the toilet, there is this other toilet thing.

VERONICA: Progress. I'll explain later.

(The lights come back up.)

VERONICA: There it is. Not under attack. It would be terrible if on your first night here my father and company decided to return and take back their property.

SONIA: They already tried and failed.

VERONICA: That won't stop them from trying again. Help them with the bags. He was a bellboy at my father's hotel. You were very good, with that cute little uniform you used to have to wear. I have a picture of it somewhere.

SONIA: Oh, please show it to me.

VERONICA: I will. Your eyes looking down. Those beautiful brown eyes. Even someone's eye color can change.

(MANUEL *lifts a bag but ends up hurting his back.*)

MANUEL: Ahhh!

ERNESTO: Are you all right?

SONIA: Have you ever had someone walk on your back?

MANUEL: On purpose?

SONIA: I read it in some sex manual. It works for back pain as well.

MANUEL: I'm sure but—

(*Even before* MANUEL *has time to say anything else,* SONIA *has pushed him to the ground.*)

SONIA: Now just close your eyes.

MANUEL: Look just let go—

SONIA: You have to trust me.

ERNESTO: She won't hurt him.

VERONICA: Whatever she does is fine with me.

(SONIA *walks on* MANUEL's *back.*)

MANUEL: Ohh...

SONIA: How do you feel? You're holding a lot in.

VERONICA: You can tell?

MANUEL: This is silly.

SONIA: A lot of anger.

MANUEL: Yes.

SONIA: You're angry we're moving in and taking half your house.

MANUEL: Not half. How many times do I have to tell you to look at the plans.

SONIA: Shhh.

MANUEL: Ahhh. Ahhhh. Ohhhh. That's enough.

VERONICA: Do you feel better?

MANUEL: You read this in a sex manual?

SONIA: I don't read. It was illustrated.

ERNESTO: Sonia got in a lot of trouble when she was young.

SONIA: Life in the provinces.

VERONICA: What about it?

SONIA: Not much to do.

VERONICA: In Havana there's something to do every minute of the day.

SONIA: I'm sure of it. We can be friends and you can show me.

VERONICA: Good. I can use the excitement.

ERNESTO: Is that what you want?

VERONICA: I haven't been excited in a while.

ERNESTO: You have a baby on the way—

VERONICA: Twins.

SONIA: How many months?

VERONICA: Ask the father.

MANUEL: Five.

VERONICA: Seven. Now I'm starting to think it wasn't you that night.

MANUEL: Stop it.

SONIA: Can I listen to the babies?

VERONICA: Not very vocal yet.

SONIA: You're happy?

VERONICA: It's going to turn out all right for them.

SONIA: Has it not turned out all right for you?

VERONICA: I've done fine.

SONIA: You haven't moved up like we have.

VERONICA: No. I guess if you're looking at it that way—

SONIA: What other way is there?

VERONICA: I think there's another way. I'm convinced there is.

SONIA: I can hear them kicking! They're restless. Like you. I want to be your friend.

VERONICA: You can come watch T V on my side of the house if you'd like.

SONIA: I would love that.

VERONICA: When my husband is away. It's not color. He promised me color.

MANUEL: I've tried.

SONIA: Color television?

VERONICA: Yes. Another broken promise.

(ROSARIO *is heard offstage.*)

ROSARIO: *(Offstage)* Anyone home. *Compañeros.*

MANUEL: What's she doing here?

ROSARIO: *(Offstage)* Where are you?

(ROSARIO *enters holding a basket full of mangos.*)

ROSARIO: Welcome, *compañeros.* My name is Rosario Cruz and I am—

MANUEL: The neighborhood spy.

ROSARIO: Fidel's eyes and ears. So he may go to bed at night—and do whatever he does very well I'm sure—and not fear a Yankee surprise attack.

MANUEL: Like the last one.

ROSARIO: Fidel wasn't surprised. Why do you think we won? I'd like to think it was because of people like me.

ERNESTO: I'm Ernesto and this is my granddaughter, Sonia.

ROSARIO: The Communist Party welcomes you to Havana. *(She hugs* SONIA. *Very official)* Accept our condolences for the grave loss you've suffered. Your mother and father made the ultimate sacrifice for our country. We will never forget them.

(ROSARIO *holds the mangos right in front of* SONIA.)

SONIA: *(Not quite sure what to do or say, she accepts the basket.)* Thanks.

VERONICA: I'm sorry.

ROSARIO: The basket is a gift from Comrade Felipe Torres and the Housing Authority...and Fidel Castro, of course.

MANUEL: Fidel Castro himself. When does he have the time?

ROSARIO: I picked the juiciest, tastiest, most succulent mangos for you, Sonia. The same ones he would have picked. Now you've arrived at the start of Carnival. The next few days will be very exciting.

SONIA: Is Carnival still on?

ROSARIO: We have blackouts but Fidel never cancels a party. Go out tonight and have fun.

ERNESTO: She's planning to.

ROSARIO: Whatever I can do for you, just let me know.

ERNESTO: We're very happy with what we've got.

(MANUEL *picks up a suitcase and exits.* ERNESTO *then follows him out.*)

ROSARIO: Your husband doesn't want me visiting, but I didn't cost him his job.

SONIA: What happened?

ROSARIO: Her husband thinks I got him fired. You should tell him the truth.

SONIA: No. Definitely not. Men don't know what to do with the truth. They either get really quiet and pretend they never heard it or they react violently.

ROSARIO: Women process it first then react violently.

VERONICA: Not all women.

ROSARIO: More and more nowadays. The Revolution has given us the right to say how we feel.

SONIA: She's right. I can challenge the authority of the husband.

VERONICA: You're not married.

SONIA: I've been around enough marriages to know what it's like.

ROSARIO: I listen in on conversations all the time. Most of the women on this block are no longer afraid of their husbands.

VERONICA: I've never feared my husband.

ROSARIO: You've never challenged him.

VERONICA: I haven't had the need to.

(SONIA *eats a mango.*)

SONIA: Mmm. Delicious.

VERONICA: How old are you?

SONIA: Nineteen. But I haven't lived a protected life.

VERONICA: You suppose I have.

SONIA: You trust him.

VERONICA: I don't trust you.

SONIA: Why are women always willing to trust the husband and never the other woman.

ROSARIO: We all know what we're capable of.

VERONICA: What do you mean?

SONIA: If the opportunity arose I'd take it.

VERONICA: What opportunity?

SONIA: To sleep with your husband.

(Short pause)

SONIA: I feel like I've been naughty and I'm being sent to my room. *(She takes the rest of the mangos with her. She takes a bite out of the one she has in her hand.)* It does taste just like one Fidel would pick.

(SONIA exits. The two women look at each other. ROSARIO opens her arms but VERONICA walks away.)

VERONICA: Do you want something to drink?

ROSARIO: You don't have to be polite.

VERONICA: Why are you here?

ROSARIO: Are you scared of me?

VERONICA: You don't come around.

ROSARIO: When the secret police raided your house I thought you'd blame me for it.

VERONICA: The more you stayed away the more—

ROSARIO: I didn't want them to think I was—

VERONICA: A friend?

(Short pause)

ROSARIO: Every day I'd look for an excuse to come in and just as I'd get to the door I'd turn around.

VERONICA: I saw you at the market.

ROSARIO: Yes. I saw you. Those avocados you're picking are not very good.

VERONICA: You look at what I buy.

ROSARIO: Out of my concern for you.

VERONICA: You're spying on me.

ROSARIO: No.

(Pause)

VERONICA: How do you like your work?

ROSARIO: I got a promotion at the factory. Now I read the newspapers to the workers while they roll the tobacco. They're very kind. They tell me I have a voice for radio. I tell them that anything's possible.

VERONICA: You know how to read.

ROSARIO: I take classes at night.

VERONICA: Since when?

ROSARIO: A few months ago.

VERONICA: And you already know how to read?

ROSARIO: Of course not. It doesn't make sense. None of what's happening makes much sense. That's what I'm trying to tell you.

VERONICA: I know.

ROSARIO: I've missed you, Veronica.

VERONICA: I've missed you.

ROSARIO: Why can't we be friends again?

VERONICA: Friends?

ROSARIO: Yes. There was a time we were—

VERONICA: We were never friends. I realize that now.

ROSARIO: I felt close to you.

VERONICA: You felt responsible for me. Not the same thing. Are you now willing to be my friend?

ROSARIO: I didn't do anything to hurt you.

VERONICA: I know that.

ROSARIO: I want to start over.

(ROSARIO *and* VERONICA *hug.*)

VERONICA: Will they ever trust me again?

ROSARIO: Yes.

VERONICA: How?

ROSARIO: I don't know yet.

VERONICA: I want them to trust me again.

(MANUEL *enters.*)

MANUEL: You can visit them on their side of the house if you want.

ROSARIO: I have to go change for Carnival. This year I'm dancing the mambo with a Soviet engineer on a float constructed completely out of tobacco leaves.

VERONICA: Let's hope your passion doesn't set it on fire.

ROSARIO: Are you kidding. Let's hope it does. (*She exits.*)

MANUEL: The old man is dragging your grandmother's chest out into the hallway to make room for their things.

VERONICA: Did you stop him?

MANUEL: The chest has no value to him. Who understands that kind of thing anymore.

VERONICA: Antiques?

MANUEL: Yes.

VERONICA: You certainly didn't when I married you. You wanted to throw it away. At least he wants to exile it to the hallway.

MANUEL: I've learned the value of things.

VERONICA: You have?

MANUEL: Yes. There is an inherent value to things old. They contain within them years and years of survival.

VERONICA: There's great value in survival.

MANUEL: Yes.

VERONICA: You mean your own survival.

MANUEL: Ours. I don't want them on our side of the house. You understand?

VERONICA: She lost her parents. You haven't had that happen to you.

MANUEL: You understand her?

VERONICA: Yes.

MANUEL: You trust them.

VERONICA: Can I trust you?

MANUEL: What do you mean?

VERONICA: What is a marriage without trust.

MANUEL: Do you have something to say?

VERONICA: I'll go see how they're doing.

MANUEL: Veronica?

VERONICA: Yes?

MANUEL: I need to know that I can—that you're still on my side.

VERONICA: Let me finish with them.

MANUEL: I can't live here—I want to go.

VERONICA: Where?

MANUEL: I can't make the same kind of money here—

VERONICA: Where do you want to go, Manuel? *(Pause. She laughs.)* Oh, yes, my father would love that. Turn to him and say you were right all along.

MANUEL: I can ask for forgiveness.

VERONICA: The kind of family I come from never forgives. I include myself in that.

MANUEL: If you admit they're right they do.

VERONICA: Did you hear me? I include myself in that.

MANUEL: I work seventy hours a week pouring cement. And there's a man across the street watching us almost every day. This isn't what I bought into.

VERONICA: It will all pass.

MANUEL: No one thought it would turn out this way. Not even you.

VERONICA: I gave up my family.

MANUEL: I've given a man some money.

VERONICA: What?

MANUEL: An old friend of mine. He's agreed to help us get out.

VERONICA: You didn't tell me anything.

MANUEL: You would have convinced me not to. You convinced me to stay once already. You would have done it again.

(VERONICA goes to the box and checks if her father's checks are still there. They're not.)

MANUEL: The dollar still has value with certain people.
It was the only money we had. Veronica?

VERONICA: In the end my father got what he wanted.

MANUEL: I lost my job and all I do now—it's
backbreaking work and for what... all because you
read books that tell you life should be a certain way.
It isn't. I've lived in the real world. You haven't. In here.
Locked up with books—theories and ideals and—this
is not what life is. I'll pay your father back.

VERONICA: He doesn't really care about the money. He
just wanted the checks cashed. You proved him right.

MANUEL: There are strangers moving in. It's only going
to get worse.

(VERONICA *sits down.*)

VERONICA: It's already dark. I never went out after
dark. How does my father go from protecting me to
leaving me behind? Right up to the last moment I never
thought he'd leave. I've never been very smart about
people—men.

MANUEL: You don't understand what it's like to marry
a woman who can be better taken care of by her father.

VERONICA: If that mattered to you, you should have
married another woman.

MANUEL: I lied but only to protect you from the real
world.

VERONICA: Is that why you didn't ask him for me?

MANUEL: Who?

VERONICA: Pepin. I would have done anything to work
with you in this real world of yours.

MANUEL: I know you would have but—

VERONICA: Why didn't you ask him?

MANUEL: I did.

VERONICA: You never did.

MANUEL: Of course I did.

VERONICA: He said you didn't.

MANUEL: He was lying.

VERONICA: Why would he lie to me?

MANUEL: It's so easy!

(Pause)

VERONICA: Yes. It is.

(Pause)

MANUEL: I didn't ask because I didn't want you going out there and getting hurt.

VERONICA: A man's world.

MANUEL: Not your world.

VERONICA: Your world?

MANUEL: Rosario's world. Sonia's.

VERONICA: Yours?

MANUEL: It was.

VERONICA: What was I going to do here?

MANUEL: You have trouble finding your way home.

VERONICA: All I wanted was for you to show me. Do you understand that everything I valued in you— your politics—you never really had any, did you? Your honesty? You married me for my family. Your dreams...whatever they might have been...all that is gone. Even your looks. I don't find you attractive anymore.

MANUEL: You don't mean that.

VERONICA: The first time I brought you home to meet my father you were wearing a jacket you'd bought stolen from a bellboy at another hotel. You took the patch off but it didn't matter. He recognized the hotel.

MANUEL: He had a keen eye for detail.

VERONICA: No. For frauds. That ability—it didn't come so easy to me. I think what I dislike most about you is that you've made me discover that I had my father in me all along. You are a fraud, Manuel.

(MANUEL *turns to go.*)

VERONICA: I had to sleep with Pepin to get you that job.

MANUEL: You don't mean that.

VERONICA: Did you really believe you could get anything on your own?

MANUEL: While I was working—

VERONICA: Yes. Right here. On our floor. You're standing in the middle of it.

MANUEL: You couldn't even do that well.

VERONICA: That's not why you lost the job.

MANUEL: No?

VERONICA: I told him the truth.

MANUEL: What truth?

VERONICA: I told him that I did your work—that you weren't smart enough to do it all by yourself. You don't know me as well as you think you do.

(MANUEL *sits down.*)

(*Pause*)

(*After a moment, several loud explosions are heard.* MANUEL *hits the floor.*)

VERONICA: (*Softly*) My father.

MANUEL: Get down.

VERONICA: He's come back.

(MANUEL *pulls a lamp down. It breaks. Semidarkness. Another explosion)*

MANUEL: They're attacking.

(MANUEL *gets* VERONICA *down on the floor next to him.)*

VERONICA: Go out there.

MANUEL: No.

VERONICA: Go. Fight for me for once.

MANUEL: Stay down.

VERONICA: You said you weren't afraid—

MANUEL: I am.

VERONICA: Coward.

MANUEL: I can't take this anymore.

(SONIA *enters. She runs up to the window and looks out.)*

SONIA: Come and look.

MANUEL: Get away from there.

VERONICA: My father—

SONIA: What are you doing? Get over here.

VERONICA: He's come back.

SONIA: It's beautiful.

MANUEL: They're shooting at us—

SONIA: Explosions.

MANUEL: Get down.

SONIA: It's Carnival! They're lighting fireworks.

MANUEL: What?

SONIA: They're celebrating.

VERONICA: Oh.

SONIA: Look at the fireworks.

(VERONICA *joins* SONIA *near the window.*)

VERONICA: Red. And more red. And some more red.
The color this year is red.

(VERONICA *goes to exit.* MANUEL *is sitting on the floor.*)

MANUEL: Where are you going?

VERONICA: I always thought that all those revolutionary
books would change the way people think. That people
would look at me not as a woman from a wealthy
family but as one with no past. That you would look
at me not as your wife but as your equal. That you
would trust I'd find my way home—it might take me
hours but I would eventually come home. What a fool
I've been.

(VERONICA *exits. Several more explosions are heard.*
A carnival is heard outside.)

SONIA: Makes my heart pound.

MANUEL: Loud noise.

SONIA: Anticipation. *(She walks up to him.)* Neutral
territory.

MANUEL: What?

SONIA: This room. Communal. Your wife doesn't trust
me.

MANUEL: I don't trust you.

SONIA: You? Your wife I understand. She wants to be
sure you stick around for the babies. I know what that's
like. I've had to call it quits after three months. The
father would not own up. You would, wouldn't you?

MANUEL: Own up. Yes. Of course.

SONIA: A gentleman.

MANUEL: I take responsibility for my actions.

SONIA: Sex is not an action one should take responsibility for. It's just an instinct.

MANUEL: I take responsibility for my instincts.
(He turns to go.)

SONIA: What was life like B C?

MANUEL: What?

SONIA: We have an expression in the provinces. B C—Before Castro. History now starts with Fidel.

MANUEL: It will end with him as well.

SONIA: How did you meet your wife?

MANUEL: I saw her at the hotel one day and followed her home.

SONIA: And to what an impressive home.

MANUEL: Those were impressive times.

SONIA: And now all the fun is indoors.

MANUEL: I wouldn't know.

SONIA: I've come to the city for privacy. You can't do anything in the country without having everyone know about it.

MANUEL: You can't do anything in this country without having Rosario know about it.

SONIA: She likes me.

MANUEL: It doesn't mean she won't turn you in.

SONIA: My affairs are of a more private matter.

MANUEL: She doesn't care.

SONIA: I kissed Rosario in my room. It's good to have something on someone. Now I can get on with the business of setting Havana on fire.

MANUEL: This is how it all works now.

SONIA: Yes.

MANUEL: You have it all figured out. My wife doesn't.

SONIA: As long as you do.

MANUEL: What do you want?

SONIA: I haven't made up my mind yet.

MANUEL: About what?

SONIA: Whether I want you or your wife. I'll let you know when I decide.

MANUEL: My wife is not the kind of woman—

SONIA: Everything is up for grabs now. Everything.

(*Offstage we hear a sewing machine.*)

MANUEL: What is that?

SONIA: My grandfather found your sewing machine.

MANUEL: Does he sew?

SONIA: He doesn't. Whenever he's confused he turns one on. The sound comforts him.

(MANUEL *and* SONIA *listen to the sewing.*)

(*Lights fade to black*)

Scene Three

(Ballet Nacional de Cuba. The lobby)

(From inside we hear Giselle *being performed.* PEPIN *enters the lobby quickly followed by* VERONICA.*)*

VERONICA: I thought the ballet's days were numbered.

PEPIN: What do you want?

VERONICA: I saw you across the aisle. Is that your wife?

PEPIN: She's a Soviet diplomat.

VERONICA: My father said it was only a matter of time before we'd be in bed with the Russians. The time has come?

PEPIN: I don't understand why you're here. I asked you to stop that day. You gave me information and I had to act on it. Otherwise, it could have cost me my job.

USHER: *(Offstage)* Shhhh!

VERONICA: What is it about the ballet?

PEPIN: What about it?

VERONICA: It's a part of the old world that's managed to survive.

PEPIN: The prima ballerina is almost blind. Every time she takes a leap, she's trusting someone will be there to catch her. It's not a question of old world or new... are you willing to take that leap?

VERONICA: I did.

PEPIN: Then trust that the Revolution will catch you.

VERONICA: I'm still falling.

PEPIN: But you haven't yet hit the floor.

VERONICA: It feels like I have.

PEPIN: Believe me, you'd know. *(He turns to go.)*

VERONICA: Can I ask you something?

PEPIN: Return to your seat, Veronica. You're missing a terrific performance.

VERONICA: Have you found someone to take my place?

PEPIN: Your place?

VERONICA: Tuesdays.

PEPIN: I decided I needed a day of rest—my week was full enough.

USHER: *(Offstage) Silencio.*

VERONICA: People have moved in with us.

PEPIN: I don't understand why you insist on having a conversation with me. It never lead any place good.

VERONICA: Did you have something to do with those people coming in?

PEPIN: No. Well yes. My actions that day may have had something to do—

VERONICA: I'm not leaving.

PEPIN: What is that?

(VERONICA has a letter in her hand.)

VERONICA: I made a list of everything I have in my house that I no longer need. I want you to come and take those things from me.

PEPIN: That's not my job.

VERONICA: Just do me that one favor.

(PEPIN goes to open the letter.)

VERONICA: Don't look at it now.

PEPIN: You want me to take your things?

VERONICA: I want to prove to you that I can let go.

PEPIN: This won't necessarily help you.

(PEPIN *starts to put the letter away. She reaches for it, then lets it go. It's clumsy. They end up touching one another. He puts the note away.*)

(PEPIN *goes.*)

(*Blackout*)

Scene Five

(*A week later*)

(ERNESTO *and* VERONICA *are on stage drinking café.*)

ERNESTO: Are you sure you should be drinking café?

VERONICA: The babies like it. Whenever I do I feel them move around inside me.

ERNESTO: When Sonia was eight months old she used to love for me to dunk her pacifier in my café. She couldn't get enough of it. She'd just lie there trying to squeeze as much of the café out of it as possible. When she could speak it was a whole different thing— then she'd demand her cup in the morning. That's when it started.

VERONICA: (*Not listening*) What?

ERNESTO: Are you all right?

VERONICA: What were you saying?

ERNESTO: Sonia's demands. I gave into every single one of them.

VERONICA: Including moving here?

ERNESTO: You can see that I'm not a happy man.

VERONICA: You didn't live your whole life in a city—
it must be difficult.

ERNESTO: She insisted we move. I couldn't say no to
her. Few people have said no to Sonia.

VERONICA: When I was growing up my life was no...
no...no.

ERNESTO: And now?

VERONICA: I've stopped asking permission.

ERNESTO: You're nervous today.

VERONICA: I see an end to this.

ERNESTO: Your pregnancy.

VERONICA: Yes. That as well.

(ROSARIO *enters.*)

ROSARIO: Good morning, compañero.

ERNESTO: Would you like some?

ROSARIO: I can't say no to café. (*To* VERONICA
Is he here?

(VERONICA *takes* ROSARIO *to one side.*)

VERONICA: What have I done?

ROSARIO: Where is he?

VERONICA: In the bedroom.

ROSARIO: They're on their way.

VERONICA: Do you think I did the right thing?

ROSARIO: Yes. Yes.

VERONICA: What is he going to say?

ERNESTO: *Compañera.*

(ROSARIO *takes a sip of café.* VERONICA *walks over to
the curtains and peeks outside.*)

ROSARIO: Mmmm. Put a little zip in my life.

ERNESTO: I make it stronger than most people.

ROSARIO: You do.

ERNESTO: I'm a widower. *Café* is the only excitement I get all day.

ROSARIO: You feel the blood rush all through your body.

ERNESTO: Yes.

ROSARIO: Now that you're in Havana I'm going to make it my business to find you something more exciting than café.

ERNESTO: A new wife?

ROSARIO: I have a friend—Petuca.

ERNESTO: Petuca? What a beautiful name.

(VERONICA *takes* ROSARIO *aside.*)

VERONICA: Rosario.

ROSARIO: I'm trying to make an old man happy.

ERNESTO: I'm old? It has never occurred to me that I'm old. *(He sits in a chair.)*

VERONICA: Do you think I did the right thing?

ROSARIO: What a silly question to ask. You did what was necessary. You're a strong woman—be strong.

VERONICA: This is what they want. They'll have to trust me after this.

ROSARIO: Do you remember when your father left? At the airport. All of us were there.

VERONICA: Yes.

ROSARIO: You didn't want to kiss him goodbye but I gently pushed you forward until you had to.

VERONICA: That kiss is all I have left now.

ROSARIO: I want you to kiss your husband goodbye so you can get started with the rest of your life.

(ERNESTO *has fallen asleep.*)

ROSARIO: He fell asleep—and how proud he was of his strong café.

VERONICA: He has no idea what's going on. It's nice to be old.

ROSARIO: Believe me, it's not. My back is starting to bother me and you can forget about my knees.

VERONICA: Not to have to worry about how it's all going to turn out.

(SONIA *enters.*)

SONIA: There's a crowd outside.

VERONICA: It's alright. Everything is going to be alright.

SONIA: Two men want to have a talk with your husband.

VERONICA: Yes. Alright. (*She doesn't move.*)

ROSARIO: Do you want me to go get him?

VERONICA: No. No. Of course. I'll go. (*She doesn't move.*)

ROSARIO: Stay here.

VERONICA: No. Can you tell them to wait?

(ROSARIO *exits.*)

(VERONICA *starts to exit just as* MANUEL *enters.* SONIA *and* VERONICA *look at him. He pours himself café.*)

MANUEL: He just make this?

VERONICA: There are people outside. They want to talk to you.

MANUEL: Who?

VERONICA: Just go talk to them. I'm sure—

MANUEL: Sonia?

SONIA: I don't know.

MANUEL: Who is it?

(ROSARIO *enters.*)

MANUEL: You told them I wanted to leave.

(VERONICA *walks up to* MANUEL.)

MANUEL: You love me?

(VERONICA *kisses* MANUEL.)

MANUEL: Do you have any idea what they're going to do to me?

VERONICA: I still remember what our dreams were even—

MANUEL: Are you listening to me? *(Pause)* I want you to come outside with me.

VERONICA: What?

MANUEL: I want you to see what's going to happen to me with your own eyes.

(MANUEL *starts to take* VERONICA.)

VERONICA: No.

MANUEL: Yes.

VERONICA: No.

MANUEL: I don't want to go alone.

(MANUEL *pulls* VERONICA *gently, but she pulls free.*)

VERONICA: No.

(*After a moment,* MANUEL *exits.*)

VERONICA: Could you make sure he's okay.

(ROSARIO *exits.*)

(*A crowd is heard outside.*)

(SONIA *pours herself a cup of café.* VERONICA *stands quietly.*)

(*After a few seconds, the crowd is no longer heard.* ERNESTO *wakes up and picks up the newspaper. He reads for a moment.*)

ERNESTO: This is going to go on for another five years at the very least. It says here—

SONIA: Stop pretending you know how to read.

ERNESTO: All right. I heard it on the radio. It's the same news, isn't it?

SONIA: Just put that down.

ERNESTO: Fidel introduced a five year plan. That means he intends it to go on.

VERONICA: The Revolution.

ERNESTO: Yes. There are plans for it to continue.

SONIA: We can consider it a five year lease on our side of the house.

ERNESTO: Another five years away from the country. Away from where I belong.

SONIA: Don't be so melodramatic. You're old. The old belong wherever there are people willing to take care of them.

ERNESTO: Are you all right?

VERONICA: Ernesto, you have my father's room. I suppose my sisters are taking care of him now. When I was young, I used to cut across the patio so that Rosario wouldn't see me—right across the patio to his room. I'd wake him up every morning. Then after the kisses and the hugs, I'd march back across the patio all sleepy eyed, back to my bed. I felt it was my duty to wake my father up. (*Pause*) My husband will get five years as well. Everyone is getting a five year extension on this life.

ERNESTO: If I make it that long. *(He gets up to go.)* I sleep on the floor out of respect for your father's property—his bed.

VERONICA: You don't have to do that.

ERNESTO: What if he were to come back and find a stranger in his bed?

SONIA: *Goldilocks and the Three Bears.* I used to love that story when I was young.

ERNESTO: What did the bears do when they found Goldilocks?

SONIA: I don't remember? Did they eat her?

VERONICA: That's *Little Red Riding Hood.*

SONIA: That was the wolf.

VERONICA: Yes.

ERNESTO: Goldilocks had tasted all three porridges and tested all three beds searching for what she liked best, but I don't know what happened when the bears came home. I imagine they were mad as hell. Wouldn't you be? *(He exits.)*

VERONICA: Isn't it funny how you can forget something that meant so much to you growing up.

SONIA: Fairy tales.

VERONICA: No. Those early morning walks across the patio. Duty. The duty toward my family.

SONIA: Do you miss them?

VERONICA: I didn't for a long time, but no matter what I do they're all around me. I don't want memory to determine my future. Maybe I should move out. Funny thing is growing up I didn't want to be here.

SONIA: Where did you want to go?

VERONICA: I saw a postcard of a town covered in snow. Salt Lake City—Mormon Capital of the World. And I knew that's where I belonged. Papi, I want to be a Mormon and go walk on clouds.

SONIA: How old were you?

VERONICA: Five. My father, the realist, told me it was really water they were walking on. Well even better, I said. He smiled, took me to a nearby lake, and threw me in. He teased me, wanted to know if I could really walk, and as much as I tried I couldn't. At that time my father was very nationalistic. Nothing was better than this country and he was going to prove it to me.

SONIA: He did.

VERONICA: This is it. I either sink or swim.

SONIA: You swam.

VERONICA: Do you think it's enough? That I've proved myself to them?

SONIA: They won't leave you alone forever.

VERONICA: Next time around it might be you they come for.

SONIA: They might come for me, but they'll end up taking you. I'm not as easy as your husband.

(VERONICA *walks over to the window.*)

VERONICA: He's still there.

SONIA: Who?

VERONICA: The man watching the house.

SONIA: Turning your husband in won't make him go away.

VERONICA: He saw me looking at him.

(ERNESTO *enters.*)

ERNESTO: I couldn't fall asleep thinking about
Goldilocks. Finally I remembered what happened.
In fact, no one knows what happened to Goldilocks.
The story ends with her jumping out the window and
whether she broke her neck or got lost in the woods or
maybe even made it out of the woods, nobody knows.
All that's certain is the three bears never saw her again.

(*Blackout*)

Scene Five

(*Five months later*)

(PEPIN, *no longer in uniform, is on stage. He peeks under the
sheet covering the chandelier. After a moment,* VERONICA
enters holding a book.)

VERONICA: What are you doing?

PEPIN: I let myself in.

VERONICA: Haven't you always.

PEPIN: You knew I would come.

VERONICA: I can't say I'm surprised.

PEPIN: Beautiful.

VERONICA: That old thing.

PEPIN: There's nothing in the law that says we don't
accept beauty.

VERONICA: What do you mean?

PEPIN: Uncover it. Let it light the room.

VERONICA: People will talk.

PEPIN: Yes. It's hard to get past that.

VERONICA: You didn't come here to tell me that.

PEPIN: No. Obviously not. I see you're reading once again.

VERONICA: Yes. Trying to build up a library. Marx. Engels. Lenin. No Proust.

PEPIN: Anything interesting?

VERONICA: It used to be you who would quote me Lenin.

PEPIN: I'm ready to listen.

VERONICA: Alright. Marx says, "Our bourgeois, not content with having the wives and daughters of their proletarians at their disposal, not to speak of common prostitutes, take the greatest pleasure in seducing each other's wives."

PEPIN: Marx said that?

VERONICA: It seems Marx would consider you bourgeois.

PEPIN: You're taking it out of context, Veronica.

VERONICA: That's what this whole thing is.

PEPIN: What?

VERONICA: Taking an idea that is pure and corrupting it until it gets you what you want.

PEPIN: That has to change.

VERONICA: Would you like something to drink.

PEPIN: You're hopelessly polite.

VERONICA: I've learned to use poison.

PEPIN: Then I'll pass.

VERONICA: It's quite easy really. All you need is trust.

PEPIN: What?

VERONICA: The trust of the person you're poisoning.

PEPIN: Trust is so hard to come by nowadays.

VERONICA: I heard rum is even harder to come by.

PEPIN: Vodka?

VERONICA: Don't care for it.

PEPIN: I adapt.

VERONICA: I try to.

PEPIN: I should compliment you.

VERONICA: On what?

PEPIN: The boys. Girls would be more difficult.

VERONICA: Why do you think that is?

PEPIN: It's easier to break their hearts.

VERONICA: I see that the revolution hasn't made you any less sexist.

PEPIN: Tolerance is an acquired taste.

VERONICA: Like vodka.

PEPIN: Vodka goes down smoother.

(Pause)

VERONICA: I should get back to them. If I don't keep my eye on them they're liable to start their own revolution.

PEPIN: With more success than this one I hope.

VERONICA: What do you mean?

PEPIN: Your application for work at the Ministry found its way to my desk. You impressed a lot of people.

VERONICA: I changed my name.

PEPIN: Yes. The address looked familiar. I drove by and I put it all together.

VERONICA: I wanted to work doing what I thought I was good at.

PEPIN: Did you think you could get a job at the Ministry without me finding out.

VERONICA: I wanted to see you again.

PEPIN: You could have come to my office.

VERONICA: I wanted you to come here.

PEPIN: Why?

VERONICA: I wanted you to experience just how empty this place is.

PEPIN: Of course the books are gone. And the chandelier—

VERONICA: Empty. Nothing to do with missing books. Empty.

PEPIN: Your husband—

VERONICA: Empty.

PEPIN: I know. The Revolution does things with...enthusiasm.

VERONICA: Enthusiasm.

PEPIN: I recommended you come work for us.

VERONICA: You did?

PEPIN: Part of a Revolution is learning, growing.

VERONICA: Really?

PEPIN: Yes. I wanted you to come work for us.

VERONICA: What—what do you mean?

PEPIN: It cost me my job. I'm afraid neither of us has a job at the Ministry of Culture. Someone higher than me accused me of bad judgment. They became suspicious of me. They investigated my background—a very thorough investigation. They discovered that my entire week was full of afternoon appointments. And that's

not all. Anyway, none of us can survive that kind of
scrutiny.

VERONICA: You didn't fight back.

PEPIN: No use. I just have to wait.

VERONICA: For what?

PEPIN: They're slowly learning. I'm sorry. They haven't
yet learned what to do with those of us who are
genuine.

VERONICA: Us?

PEPIN: With those of you who are genuine. It's a lesson
we'll have to learn if this is going to work. *(He starts to
go.)* Why don't you turn that light on once in a while.

VERONICA: What?

PEPIN: It really is a beautiful thing. *(After a moment,
he exits.)*

*(VERONICA looks at the chandelier. It's as if she's looking at
it for the first time. SONIA enters and VERONICA is startled.)*

VERONICA: Where are the babies? Did they take the
babies? What happened—

SONIA: Shh. They're asleep.

VERONICA: Oh. I thought—

SONIA: No one is going to take them away.

VERONICA: I had a nightmare last night. It was so real.
The man across the street had come over and taken
my babies.

SONIA: Mariano. I found out his name.

VERONICA: The man across the street.

SONIA: He has a name. Mariano. I flirt with him every
day.

VERONICA: How could you talk to him?

SONIA: He's harmless, really. He doesn't even know why he's standing there. They just told him to keep an eye on us.

VERONICA: Just another gossip.

SONIA: Yes.

VERONICA: My grandmother used to watch the neighbors make love from her room.

SONIA: She did?

VERONICA: She watched everything they did.

SONIA: Your grandmother would have done well working for this government.

VERONICA: Not much difference.

SONIA: When I was walking home from the doctor's yesterday with the babies, I caused a scandal. They thought I was a single mother, tried to make me feel ashamed. Do you think Havana will change?

VERONICA: What do you mean?

SONIA: That perhaps one day women will be allowed to be women. That we'll get to do what we want.

VERONICA: And I didn't even think you were a revolutionary.

SONIA: It's so easy.

VERONICA: I don't think so.

SONIA: No. It is. It's not giving a damn. For now, I'll continue with my scandals.

VERONICA: What's your next scandal?

SONIA: Mariano's seduction. He's married so I know the type.

(Crying is heard offstage.)

VERONICA: Is someone trying to take them?

(VERONICA *goes to exit but* ERNESTO *walks in holdin
both babies.*)

ERNESTO: They insisted I pick them up—kind of
reminded me of you.

SONIA: Really?

ERNESTO: Their demands.

SONIA: They're so cute. Oh, before I forget. Here.
(*She takes out a letter.*)

VERONICA: From my father. It's opened.

SONIA: Mariano read it.

VERONICA: He did?

SONIA: He didn't read one word before Fidel, and now
he reads his neighbors letters. If that's not proof the
revolution works, I don't know what is.

ERNESTO: What does it say? Is he coming back. Do we
have to move out?

SONIA: I don't think our half of the house is his
anymore.

ERNESTO: What does it say? Is he coming to kick us out?

SONIA: You can't worry. If he comes back Fidel will kick
him out again.

VERONICA: Why don't you read me the letter, Ernesto.

(VERONICA *gives* ERNESTO *the letter. The lights shift—
very slowly. At first,* ERNESTO *has trouble reading it,
but as the lights shift he grows in confidence.*)

ERNESTO: "Every day Havana fades so that the streets
I played in when I was a child are now alleys. Memory
either narrows a place to the point of disappearing
or causes it to grow in your imagination. I can tell you
that in the memory of most of my friends, Havana has
only grown. They want Havana. I've decided to let go

because for me Havana is a house on a quiet street,
a house that no longer belongs fully to me. Street by
street, room by room, they've taken Havana from me.
Last night I forgot what you look like; and though
the thought of forgetting you rattled me a little, I soon
decided that you are like the house that no longer
belongs to me. With love, your Father. P S: This is
my last letter to you. I have grown sentimental, and
I am embarrassed by everything I say or do in regards
to Cuba."

(Pause)

VERONICA: I love you, Father.

ERNESTO: Yes.

VERONICA: Do you love me, Father?

ERNESTO: Yes.

VERONICA: With all your heart?

ERNESTO: Yes.

VERONICA: Say it, Father.

ERNESTO: With all my heart.

(The babies begin to cry. The lights change back.)

VERONICA: You are my family. We are a family.

SONIA: Of course.

VERONICA: Invite him in for café.

SONIA: Who?

VERONICA: Mariano from across the street.

SONIA: I don't know if he can cross the street.

VERONICA: If he can read, I'm sure he can cross the
street.

SONIA: I don't know if he's allowed to.

VERONICA: Why not try. Let's have a party.

SONIA: What are we celebrating?

VERONICA: Let's just have a party. After a while, we'll know exactly what we're celebrating.

(VERONICA *turns on the chandelier. For the first time in the play, it's on. A brilliant light covers the entire stage.*)

SONIA: It's wonderful.

VERONICA: It's enchanting. Close the curtains. Hurry.

(*As* SONIA *and* VERONICA *start to close the curtains, the lights start to change.*)

ERNESTO: Like a fantasy.

VERONICA: Yes. It's like that, isn't it.

SONIA: Our own little world.

VERONICA: Our own special place.

(*The babies continue to cry.*)

ERNESTO: Show the babies the light.

(*They do. They stand in front of the light, closer now than ever. They're a new family.*)

VERONICA: If they ever come back, the man who wrote that letter and his friends, we'll close all our doors, turn off the lights, and hope they don't recognize their old homes. This is ours now. No one's going to take it away.

(*The babies stop crying. Everyone laughs.*)

(*Lights fade to black*)

END OF PLAY